The Power of
Acknowledgment

The Power of Acknowledgment

Judith W. Umlas

IIL PUBLISHING, NEW YORK

IIL Publishing, New York titles may be purchased in bulk at a discount for educational, business, fund-raising, or sales promotional use. For information, please e-mail michelle.blackley@iil.com or call 212-515-5144.

Published by IIL Publishing, New York, a division of International Institute for Learning, Inc., 110 East 59th Street, 31st Floor, New York, NY 10022
www.iil.com

Design: Tony Meisel

ISBN 0-97082-764-4

Printed in the United States of America

Dedication

This book is dedicated first of all to my soul sis-
ter and cherished friend, Barbara Leach-Kelly.
She was one who truly knew, understood and used the
power of acknowledgment every day of her life, many
times each day. Barbara, your acknowledgments and
your deep, abiding love for me have put me on the path
I am traveling today, and help to keep me there. I thank
you for all you have given me, and I hope I am able to
pass your gift on to others.

I also dedicate this book to my wonderful and always
evolving family: my funny, romantic, adorable and, above
all, supportive husband Bob Umlas; my awesomely aware,
loving and sensitive daughter, Stefanie Umlas; my ener-
getic, caring and creative son, Jared Umlas; my beautiful parents—always full of love and acknowledgment
and continuous support for me—Dr. Paul and Sylvia

Wagreich; and my brother Dr. Carl Wagreich, whose humanitarian pursuits and contributions are a constant inspiration, and whose love and commitment mean the world to me.

I am a lucky person to have chosen this family and to have had them choose me!

In love and light,
Judy

Contents

Introduction

What actions would you take if you knew with absolute certainty that a simple action you *could* take every day for no cost and little effort would change your world, and the world at large, dramatically and profoundly for the better? What if this ability is something every person on this planet possesses, yet few use much if at all? What if using it regularly would transform your relationship with your husband or wife? What if doing it would make your colleagues at work not be able to do enough for you, and make the office atmosphere vibrant, productive and alive instead of lethargic, competitive, frustrated and bored?

All of this is possible, yet most people don't recognize this incredible tool or understand its power. What all of us possess, but most of us don't use often enough, is the power of acknowledgment. Many of us have our reasons for not using it, but these are just excuses, ratio-nalizations that hold us back from achieving powerful, positive results wherever we are or go. I have written this book to help people understand and use a tool that I believe can produce profound and dramatic changes in our intimate circles and far beyond.

How have I come to this conviction? For most of my adult life I have been keenly aware of the effect that heartfelt acknowledgment has had upon the people around me. I tend to acknowledge freely, comfortably, and with appreciation the many gifts people display all the time. These gifts can be talents they have worked hard to develop, the way they present and carry themselves, their thoughtful actions, or their commitment to achieving a goal. There is no scarcity of qualities we can and should acknowledge in the people around us.

Over time, I have come to realize how difficult it is for many people to acknowledge others. I have often wished that I could find an appropriate way to clue them in to just how important it is.

For example, a medical practitioner recently told me how terrified she is of flying and how much it helps her when her husband assures her that everything will be all right just before they get on the plane. She revealed how his calmness and sense of security both relax and soothe her. "Of course I would never tell *him* that!" she said emphatically.

I was literally speechless when I heard this and couldn't even react. On my way home, though, I felt I had to step out of my role as her patient and take the risk of suggesting that she tell her husband how she felt about the contribution he makes to her life. "It will transform your relationship," I said when I reached her on my cell phone. "Will you tell him?" "Well, maybe," she said. But did she do it? I certainly hope so, but I can't say with certainty that she did. I'm not sure where this lack of desire to acknowledge another for something that we truly admire comes from, but I often see that people are reluctant to express the positive words, thoughts, or feelings that are in their hearts.

Periodically I've found myself becoming an "acknowledgment bridge" by passing along compliments I've heard to the person who was praised. Someone will say something nice to me about another person and I'll assume that this other person knows about it. Yet when I mention the compliment they have received to that person, they are usually totally surprised. "You're kidding! I had no idea!" they often tell me.

One hard-working, constantly overwhelmed co-worker of mine was amazed and relieved to discover that she was highly regarded by another, more senior co-worker. As much as she always accomplished, she often felt she was not doing enough, and it thrilled her to hear the acknowledgment. I felt sad, though, that the senior person had never acknowledged her directly. What if I hadn't passed it along? I find it unsettling that this person would not have known how much she was valued!

Passing on acknowledgments has the opposite effect of gossip, which always hurts. And somehow the "gossipee" always seems to find out about it. Being an "acknowledgment bridge," on the other hand, energizes, thrills and empowers the recipient. I pass on acknowledgments whenever I can and am always amazed at the wondrous and surprised response I encounter. But the deeper lesson is that it's even better to directly acknowledge the people we admire, respect or even envy. (In fact, as we'll see later, jealousy and acknowledgment are powerful partners).

My purpose in writing this book is to inspire you to consciously acknowledge the people around you every day—many times a day, if possible. But only acknowledge others when it's appropriate: Acknowledgment is only meaningful when it is done honestly, with good intention and delight, and with no ulterior motive.

People can smell insincerity and they will lose trust in and respect for you.

Once you start this practice, which requires paying attention to the good qualities of the people around you, you will find yourself becoming awed by their accomplishments, talents and wisdom—from a child, to an elderly person, to a sales clerk.

For example, think of the under-acknowledged security people at the airline terminals. Since September 11, 2001 they have been faced with the thankless job of making us remove our shoes, our overcoats as well as our inner jackets, our computers and nail scissors, and making sure we comply with changing restrictions. Watch them light up when you tell them that you appreciate how they are helping to protect us all from harm. I do this each time I am at an airport, and based on my experience, I predict that you will make an extraordinary difference in their day when you acknowledge them! You, too, will feel healthier, lighter, more gracious, more balanced and even more peaceful in doing so.

Imagine what it would be like in divorce court, if husbands and wives acknowledged each other for the contributions to their lives that the other had made, and how each helped the other grow and evolve as a human being—even as they were choosing to go their separate ways. I actually saw something like this happen at a service held to honor a dear friend who recently passed away. In a heartfelt eulogy, her ex-husband got up to acknowledge the incredible person she was, how deeply she had contributed to his life and how she would do so forever. No one was dry-eyed during his speech, and it challenged everything we all knew about divorce and its aftermath.

While this may sound far-fetched, starting to acknowledge all those who truly deserve it, instead of withholding our true thoughts and praise, could begin to transform the world—person by person—right before our eyes.

This book will teach you how to get those acknowledgments out of your brain (I know they're there!) and into your mouth. Keeping them inside is actually a rip-off both of ourselves and of those we could acknowledge. You and they feel wonderful when you do acknowledge them. And in Chapter 6 you'll see what research points to about the physiological and psychological ways both givers and receivers benefit from practicing this technique.

What makes me such an "expert" in this life-altering habit that I felt I had to write a book about it? When you get down to it, my expertise stems from the powerful responses I've gotten from others when I have either acknowledged them for something, or shared insights about acknowledgments from my personal experience.

Years ago I was troubled by the way people spoke to me at my job at CBS Television while I was pregnant. So I wrote an article for a major magazine entitled, "How NOT to Talk to a Pregnant Businesswoman." Overnight, I became the authority on this subject, appearing on Good Morning America and 200 radio stations, just because no one else was talking about this publicly. I had simply been venting my anger and frustration and giving some "rules" of communication that I felt would make things more workable.

My expertise in the power of acknowledgment similarly comes from being frustrated and sad when I see acknowledgment withheld, especially when I also see on a regular basis (as in every day, many times a day) the miracles that happen when you deliver it with generosity! Maybe you could say my capability in this area also comes from having worked in communications for my whole career—from CBS to PBS to cable TV, business television and now corporate learning at a global project-management training company, International Institute for Learning. But I suspect that it comes from my personal inclination, observation, experimentation and—

yes, at times—uncomfortable efforts at communication.

It's from my own experience that I know that acknowledgment is a skill we all have (although it is in need of development, like muscles that improve when you exercise). I've also seen the power of acknowledgment, how it changes the lives, the moods and the self-perception of both the giver and the recipient, each and every time it is practiced. And miraculously, it is available all the time to all of us.

I am committed to giving this power to anyone who will accept it (or giving them the tools to enhance their capabilities in this area if they already practice it) because I strongly believe that we can change the world, one person at a time as we use the power of acknowledgment to turn on the light in ourselves and others. I've seen it happen. With many of us doing this together, the positive change will occur a lot faster and the light will be a lot brighter.

One forewarning, though: as you begin to use this skill, or use it more than you did previously, you might occasionally have to acknowledge someone two or three times before he or she can really "hear" what you're saying, due to their own negative self-image or disbelief. This isn't easy or comfortable, but I will show you the best way to do this. However, most people just eat it up and melt from the acknowledgment you give them.

The principles I discuss in the pages that follow will walk you through the steps it takes to use the power of acknowledgment effortlessly and to understand how to employ it in all the different parts of your life. In doing so, you will without a doubt make the world a better, healthier, more peaceful and thrilling place for all of us.

Chapter 1

Getting Started

Principle #1: The world is full of people who deserve to be acknowledged.

It will be easier to acknowledge those you care most about if you start by practicing your acknowledgment skills on people you don't know very well, or even know at all. Then you will begin making the world a happier place.

Consider all the people you meet up with every day besides your family and co-workers: the lady at the dry cleaners, the person behind the counter at the coffee shop you go to every morning, the gas station attendant and the hundreds of others you come into contact with as you move through your life.

What would happen if you told the young woman who knows your coffee order and gets it ready as she sees you walking through the door, how awesome she is for remembering your "small, black, half decaf, half regular caramel" coffee when she has so many other customers? I know, because I've done just that: A smile broke out on her face, the tiredness disappeared from her eyes, and she exclaimed, "People don't usually take the time to say anything so nice to me!"

I have experienced this kind of reaction so often. When I get a helpful telephone operator—one who tries a bit harder than I would expect to find the number I am searching for—I have said, "I really appreciate your trying so hard to help me find the number, even when I don't have the correct spelling of the name or the person's street address!" I can actually feel the person expanding over the telephone wire as I say this. Sometimes they are dumbfounded, almost speechless. Other times they sound nearly joyful. A few have even acknowledged *me* for acknowledging them.

We just have no idea what contribution we make to someone who talks to thousands of people without any human(e) interaction, with this simple, caring act of appreciation and acknowledgment. Later on I will present you with a real life example of this phenomenon that occurred with a public employee I acknowledged, and it will knock your socks off!

Could a general lack of acknowledgment be why the world doesn't work for so many people? Why there are crimes of passion, crimes of greed, and marital tugs of war over children? Why there is widespread depression and despair among young people and seniors, as well as among many in the ages between? I believe that quite a few of the world's problems can be relieved, or at least diminished, by changing this one aspect of human behavior. I maintain that much of the world's pain comes from people feeling they are not good enough, not smart enough, and not rich enough; believing that they can never get enough of whatever it is they think they need in order to feel good about themselves. And that this is what drives them to do things that make the world seem like it is broken. Changing just this one aspect of human behavior on a colossal scale might solve many problems. And—wondrously—it is within our power to start doing this immediately within our own personal universe.

When you get down to it, much of the time people do bad things because they feel bad about themselves. And they feel bad about themselves, at least in part, because they have not been appropriately and properly acknowledged—in a way that they can truly get it—about how good they are, what they contribute to others, how they excel at various things.

Have you ever watched a small child puff up her chest when you tell her she has helped you do something? And have you ever witnessed the way another small child who is publicly berated or screamed at by a parent, shrinks into herself and becomes "insignificant"?

What if all of us started acknowledging everyone around us for the good things they do, the talents they possess, and the "gifts" they are to others? My purpose in writing this book is to suggest a way to fix this condition of perceived worthlessness that propels so many people toward destructive, harmful, uncaring actions. It begins and ends with you, if you are willing to participate. And here's how it starts—with acknowledging absolute strangers.

Why strangers? Because doing a good job of acknowledging someone can be harder than it sounds. It makes sense to try it out on people who aren't as close to you as your family, friends and co-workers—people who will be pleasantly surprised and not likely to waste time worrying about your motives. And because when you make someone's day, you both benefit. That's what happened to me when I acknowledged the retired people who operate the voting booths that give us the power to choose our leaders. When I've acknowledged the volunteers who donated many hours of their time so that I can vote, their faces lit up and they thanked me for thanking them.

And here's one of the most charming experiences of the power of acknowledgment I've seen. When my then ten-year-old daughter Stefanie and her friend Priya decided that they wanted to give manicures to all of the ladies in a nursing home—about 20 of them—they called the facility and got permission to perform their mission, as long as an adult (lucky me!) supervised their activities. After saving up their allowances for several weeks in preparation for the visit, they bought many glorious colors of nail polish, polish remover and emery boards as well as tiny journals in which they wanted to write stories from the ladies' lives—an element they had added to their powerful purpose.

On the day of our visit, I watched one lady after another—many of them memory impaired—light up, become alert and laugh joyously as Stefanie and Priya acknowledged them by painting their nails and transcribing their life stories into the journals that they then presented to them. For days afterward, Stefanie and Priya seemed to expand with their own joy each time they told someone about the ladies they had come to know and appreciate. Acknowledging someone has a positive effect not only on the person acknowledged but on the acknowledger as well. (As I said earlier, you will learn more about the psychological and physiological changes that may actually be occurring in both individuals in Chapter 6.)

So start building your acknowledgment expertise by thanking and appreciating your bus driver and telephone operator, the customer service person who actually does help you, the kid who bags your groceries at hyper speed at the supermarket, or the person who helps you find the right toner cartridge for your three-year-old computer printer. In short, anyone around us who merits praise, for actions or attributes large or small. And "everywhere" is a great place to begin practicing the skill and watching people light up as you do it!

Chapter 2

Harnessing the Power of Acknowledgment to Build Stronger Relationships

Principle #2: Acknowledgment builds intimacy and creates powerful interactions.

Acknowledge the people around you directly and fully, especially those with whom you are in an intimate relationship. What is it about your spouse, your daughter, your uncle, your oldest colleague or subordinate that you want to acknowledge? Look for ways to say how much you value them, and then be prepared for miracles!

Have you ever noticed that you are often afraid to acknowledge someone, even when you admire something that this person has done? Why do people experience this difficulty? Because it can be awkward and embarrassing if you are not practiced in this skill or art form, whatever you prefer to call it. Here's a real-life example: One day I asked a colleague whether we needed to have a subject matter expert double-check some work a certain program developer had written because it was about to be made public.

"No," she stated emphatically. "He is one of the few people about whose work I can wholeheartedly say, 'Just publish it.' He's that good!"

Later, when I thanked the program developer for the work he had done for us, I relayed my colleague's compliment to him via e-mail.

He replied, "Did she *really* say that? I hope I can live up to it, and I'll do my best to make that happen."

I could feel the smile in the e-mail and the power of the acknowledgment, even if it was secondhand.

But why hadn't my colleague acknowledged him directly? Here are a few of the reasons people give for keeping these wonderful words to themselves:

1. I don't want to cheapen my acknowledgment by praising too many people too often. It waters it down and makes it worth less.

2. People might not work as hard if they are told how good they are; worrying whether you value them makes them work harder.

3. A rare compliment is worth much more than a frequent acknowledgment; it is treasured more.

In later chapters, we will explore these three assumptions—I call them myths—individually. For now, we'll say that there is probably some element of truth in all of these statements, but not enough to make it appropriate to withhold an acknowledgment when it is truthful and sincere.

If a boss were to distribute $100 bills to employees when they did something particularly good, would those bills have less value if they were given out with great frequency? Not if the employees felt they had deserved and earned them!

I found out quite by accident that someone very close to me—my husband of 36 years at the time—was withholding acknowledgments. This happened a few years ago, when I was having a "down" day and he called me from work to check in. Bob was so sympathetic and caring that I asked if he would write me a love letter and e-mail it to me. "That would mean a lot to me and might even make me feel better," I said.

He hesitated, saying that computer "geeks"—he's a Microsoft® Excel Developer—don't write good love letters, but agreed to give it a try. Ten minutes later I was shocked to find a three-page love letter (he types fast, and thinks faster!) full of the most sincere and dear acknowledgments I had ever received from him. He mentioned loving acts I had performed for a family in our neighborhood when the mother had passed away (I thought he had hardly taken note of them) and referenced the great success of a surprise 60th anniversary party I had organized for my parents. He told me how attractive I was and much more.

I was deeply moved and my depressed mood evaporated on the spot. Later, I asked whether he had thought about those things without telling me, or if they had just occurred to him when he was trying to write the letter.

"Oh, I think those kinds of things all the time," he said somewhat sheepishly. "I just don't bother to get them from my brain to my mouth."

I read and reread his letter many times during that day, and for many days afterward. It was such a boost that I had the audacity to ask him (more as a joke than anything else) if he could write me two love letters a week. He paused, thought about it and then answered somewhat tentatively, "Well, I guess I could try ...."

Two years later, I am still receiving love letters every Monday and Thursday, unless extraordinary circumstances intervene. And I nearly always respond with my own acknowledgments of him. This practice has made our relationship more intimate and joyful than I could ever have imagined possible.

All of us have acknowledgments stored in us. As you start paying attention to them, you will be shocked at the many things you could say to the people all around you that would make their day and change their lives. You may not realize it, but you are shortchanging both yourself and them by keeping them locked away in your mind. They are your "gold" to give away, at no cost to you, with minimal effort and energy. In fact, energy comes to you as you deliver these messages and see how people respond to them.

Recently I sat a friend down over a cup of coffee with a mission in mind. She is a person who has had great challenges raising both of her children, and I wanted her to know what an outstanding mother I thought she was. She had just given something incredibly special to her teenage daughter—not anything that she had purchased, but rather two days of time to go with her on a class trip that her daughter would otherwise not have been allowed to participate in. For the mom it was just something she did. For me, it was evidence of her unshakable commitment to and love for her daughter.

As I acknowledged her deeply for what she had done, my friend first responded that it was nothing special, but when I repeated the acknowledgment, her eyes grew wide, a big smile broke out on her face, and she accepted the acknowledgment with a huge "thank you," getting teary as she said it. I was thrilled, knowing I had helped her at least a little with the challenges she continuously experienced.

Don't hold back! You can start practicing your acknowledgment skills as soon as you finish this chapter.

Chapter 3

Using Acknowledgment to Neutralize Jealousy and Envy

Principle #3: Acknowledgment neutralizes, defuses, deactivates and reduces the effect of jealousy and envy!

Acknowledge those you are jealous of, for the very attributes you envy. Watch the envy diminish and the relationship grow stronger as you grow to accept valuable input from the person you were envying.

I believe that many of the problems we face stem from envy—from personality disputes to serious crime. You might experience that nasty feeling when you see someone who's in wonderful physical shape, when yours is not that great. Or when you contemplate the person who sat in the next cubicle at your first job who has now sailed far past you professionally.

Jealousy speaks to some of our deepest wishes and fears. Ignoring it won't make it go away and it can poison your relationship with a particular person, or—if you are like me—with many people. But, if you know how to use them in concert, acknowledgment and jealousy can be powerful partners for good. Yes, you can actually use acknowledgment—when delivered freely and truthfully, and not for any tangible reward—to reduce or even eliminate this disturbing, negative emotion.

How could that be? While envy or jealousy makes us withhold anything that could make the envied person seem even better or stronger, the act of consciously acknowledging that person for those qualities actually shifts reality; you can feel the jealousy evaporate in the face of your acknowledgment. You feel it in your gut, you hear it in your voice, and you see it in the other person's face.

Jealousy, as we all know, is a potent and fierce

destroyer—or at least diminisher—of relationships. My husband, Bob and I saw this work with a close friend of ours, whom Bob has known since childhood. Aside from being a leader in mathematics education at a major university, Jerry, a Ph.D., is a whiz at finances and almost all of the other necessary practicalities of life (life insurance, taxes, and 401ks, to name a few). My husband and I found ourselves gritting our teeth and getting upset every time he talked about these areas we knew so little about.

One day, we overcame our envy and uncertainty and said, "You're so good at all of these things. Can you help us?" Of course, he was delighted to do so. Our jealousy evaporated and we were able to save a great deal of money by following his excellent financial advice. Meanwhile, our friendship became even more intimate and meaningful.

It was much harder for me to come to terms with my feelings about my dear and wise friend, Kayli, who to me embodies motherhood in its most positive form. She did not pursue a career but devoted her life instead to raising her two sons, Scott and David, who have turned out to be wonderful, charming, and unselfish.

Unlike Kayli, I have had an active career practically since my first child was born. Although I worked from home as a telecommuter for many years, my daughter was angry at what she perceived to be my lack of focus on her. One day when she was about five years old, she drew a picture of me holding a telephone in each ear and sitting in front of a computer.

While my husband and I love both of our bright, talented children absolutely, we have not had an easy time raising them. I often gazed wistfully at Kayli's family, feeling guilty for having had such an engrossing, time-consuming career while she had made a full-time commitment to her kids, displaying great creativity as well as enviable patience in parenting.

What has helped me handle these feelings and deepen our friendship is directly acknowledging Kayli's wisdom, intuition and expertise in mothering by seeking her advice. One instance stands out in my mind because it transformed my connection with Kayli and made a huge difference in my relationship with my 14-year-old son, Jared.

After a particularly difficult period in our family, I said to Kayli, "I'll bet you can think of a wonderful way for me to show how much I appreciate Jared given the rough time we have all been having."

Acknowledging Kayli in this way opened me up, without jealousy, to her wonderful advice, which I know I could not otherwise have heard. "Why don't you ask him if he would like to go on a trip with you, and where he would like to go?" she said.

I knew what the answer would be, though, and it terrified me. "He'll say Paris, France, and we don't have the vacation time or the money to go there now."

"Go anyway," she said. "It'll be the most important trip of his life."

So I asked, so he requested what I predicted he would, and that's where we went. In order to save money, we left my husband home. I took the extra vacation time, and as a result, I wrote this chapter from Paris after an outstanding day with my son on the best trip of his life and one of the best of mine.

In fact, Jared returned the gift of that trip to me many times over. For example, when I told him that the French couple I had stayed with for a summer when I was 18 years old lived fairly close by, he said he would love to meet them. Mario and Claudia, ages 81 and 87, were thrilled with the idea when I wrote to them proposing it. So they met us in Paris where we all spent two glorious days together. After they left, I presented a list of things to Jared that we could do on our last day in Paris, including taking a train to an amusement park. But he surprised me by saying he would prefer to take a train to visit Mario and Claudia in Lyon, to see where they lived and where I had spent my summer when I was a teenager. And so we did, giving me a deep sense of completion with people I have dearly loved, but rarely seen, all of these years.

If I hadn't acknowledged Kayli's wisdom, I wouldn't have been able to ask for her advice and be truly open to it. And I wouldn't have given Jared the opportunity to acknowledge me in a way that was both loving and lasting. This has finally allowed me to truly let go of my jealousy of Kayli and be able to seek and receive her advice whenever I need it. Making this constraint disappear has been a wonderful gift to both of us.

At work, the stakes can actually feel higher and riskier than with friends and family. One rather dramatic example of the acknowledgment/jealousy relationship in the workplace stands out in my mind. I had approached the president of a well-known and highly respected training institute to see if we could persuade the founder of it—a true guru and hero in the field of quality—to be the lead presenter of a live, interactive, global satellite broadcast that our company would produce and market. Though getting the founder to participate was a very long shot, we were successful in making it happen. I immediately got our marketing team to put together ideas for the brochure that we would use to let the world know about the upcoming event. The president of the institute wasn't satisfied with the concept our team came up with, though, and asked if he could do it himself (he personally had a strong design and marketing talent, as well as the passion for doing it). The brochure turned out to be outstanding—we later found out that many people actually framed it and hung it on their office walls!

As thrilled as I was with the piece, I felt threatened and envious of both his vision and the ability to carry it out. Why hadn't I been able to inspire a result like this from our marketing team? Even the fact that the broadcast turned out to be the most highly attended one in our company's history—a huge win for all of us—didn't eliminate my feelings of jealousy and inadequacy. Of course the "star" of the broadcast had a lot to do with the success, but I recognized that the brochure had made it happen in concrete dollars and cents terms.

A few months later, we needed to fill the head of marketing slot at our company. I knew of the true passions and demonstrated talents of the president of the institute I had worked with. Since I was involved in the job search, I had a crazy thought about his being a potential candidate, strange as that might have seemed to the rest of the world. At first my jealousy, as well as my fear of insulting him, kept me from broaching the subject.

Finally, I summoned up the nerve to call him and acknowledge his extraordinary design and marketing talents. I started by saying, "I hope I'm not being inappropriate in asking you this, but we have a head of marketing position open now at our company. Would you be offended if I ask you if you would like to be considered for that position?" Not only was he *not* insulted, but he was delighted at the opportunity to do what he was truly passionate about. He very quickly assumed the role of our company's head of marketing, and loved every minute of his numerous years in that role! And this gratifying result had been the amazing outcome of being able to overcome my jealousy, by acknowledging what I envied most about this person, and then making the leap from the acknowledgment to the offer. If I hadn't been able to acknowledge his talents directly, I never would have been able to consider asking him to be a candidate for that critical job.

Acknowledgment of those we are jealous of opens us to their expertise and profound wisdom and makes them eager to share their gifts with us.

Chapter 4

How Acknowledging People Produces Great Results at Work

Principle #4: Recognizing good work leads to high energy, great feelings, high-quality performance and terrific results. Not acknowledging good work causes lethargy, resentment, sorrow and withdrawal.

Recognize and acknowledge good work, wherever you find it. It's not true that people only work hard if they worry whether you value them. Quite the opposite!

Can you imagine this scene, which takes place every day all over the world? You have just completed a difficult and challenging job. Perhaps you've worked alone on a project that needed three people to complete it, and got it done before the scheduled deadline and under budget. Customers and potential customers are already telling you how much easier it makes their jobs, how excited they are, and how this new product really fills a need. You report all this to your boss and all you get is a weak and distracted, "Oh, okay."

You already know what you're left with: resentment, lack of energy, and most of all (but not usually identified) sorrow. Why did you bother to put in all of the extra hours, why did you feel the deep commitment to getting the job done even with insufficient resources? "Who cares anyway?" you ask yourself.

That's what happened to a sweet, gentle person I know who used to work around the clock at a senior-level position in a large company. His boss, however, never acknowledged his outstanding work and high-quality results. All he did was find fault with him personally and pick continuously at insignificant things.

My friend finally threw in the emotional towel. He didn't quit, but he now works a 9 to 5 day, gets the minimum job done and is very sad about it. You can see the intense pain in his eyes when he speaks of the situation; he also has a deep sense of resignation.

There is some hope, though: Others in the department who felt the same way got a committee from upper management to evaluate the boss. His lack of appreciation and acknowledgment are being addressed.

That's one way to handle this kind of situation. Wouldn't it be better and more productive, though, for managers to generously give acknowledgment when it is deserved, and for subordinates not to have to go to such lengths to get what they ought to have and truly need?

Now imagine a different kind of scenario: You go to your boss, an extremely busy multi-tasker who rarely has time to eat lunch or even go to the bathroom. You clear your throat and wait until she looks up, then speed through an update on your project, highlighting its rapid completion—under budget and before the delivery deadline—and the positive user feedback.

Your boss looks up, makes eye contact and says, "I know how hard you worked on this project, how much overtime you put in, the weekends you worked. This is a phenomenal accomplishment. Thank you for your commitment to getting the job done to the highest level of quality, even with limited resources. On the next project we'll see if we can get you more of the support you need. Great job!"

What effect would this kind of response have on your feelings of self-worth, your motivation, and your opinion of your job and the difference you make to your company? Imagine how positively you would feel and react.

I know, because nearly this exact scene took place when I worked at CBS Television. At the time, I produced short pieces for our local news broadcast—the editorials—every day. Some were filmed on location with news crews; others were done solely in a studio and taped for later broadcast.

Our editorial board had decided to do a "celebrate New York" piece which I would write and produce. I had instructed the cameraman to make it a true celebration, to be as creative and artistic as he could be. When the footage came back and I reviewed it with our editor, we put it together with the famous song, "New York, New York" from the musical "On the Town." I was so pleased with the final product that I thought our very busy Editorial Director should see it before it was broadcast.

He came down to the videotape area, viewed the two-minute piece, said he would be right back and disappeared. I was speechless, not knowing what he had thought of it and feeling that all my hard work was on the line. Was it too "cinematic" for local news? I had trusted my instincts and pulled out all the stops. Moments later, he returned with *his* boss, who was rarely seen by anyone but those in his innermost circle. My boss had the tape operator play the piece again. When it was done, both men turned to me and told me what a phenomenal, creative job it was.

Eventually they submitted the editorial for the New York Press Club's "Heart of New York Award" and it won. The acknowledgment and recognition I received inspired me to embark on many other even more challenging and creative projects, at CBS and elsewhere.

Written acknowledgments can also be very effective, with the added benefit that the employee can read them again and again—very helpful on days when things aren't going so well! They take three or four minutes to write and can mean a world of difference to your recipients. For example, it is well known that former CEO Jack Welch's celebrated, countless, hand-written notes to GE people acknowledged, inspired, and motivated them.

Here's an actual example of a written acknowledgment that lit up, energized and motivated a key sales person in our project management training company. It was in the form of an e-mail from Robin, a senior executive, acknowledging the excellent progress that she had been making. And I think we can all learn something from this person who continuously writes some of the best acknowledgments (but only when they are well-deserved) that I have ever read. Here is Robin's acknowledgment of Michelle, as well as the ensuing e-mail thread that resulted and which she has saved for several years.

Subject: Congratulations!
Hi Michelle,

Congratulations on your outstanding string of recent sizeable sales successes! You have done a masterful job with working these key accounts even in the face of considerable distractions such as (the introduction of) Six Sigma and being (our CEO's) acting secretary!

I am personally very proud of what you have managed to accomplish these past 2-3 years. I remember all those conversations we used to have when you lacked confidence and doubted your abilities to transition successfully into on-site sales and now look at you —top of the hill! I told you that you could do it! You are a great shining example to others (who should be humble enough to take note!) and I am quite sure that the entire management team is as proud of you as I am. It's great to have you as part of this team and I really look forward to working a few shows with you next year. Keep up the great work and aim ever higher—you know you can do it!

Robin

She wrote this back to him:

Robin—

Thank you so much for the beautiful e-mail. It means so much to me to receive these types of communications.

I thank you for your continued support—without you... and the rest of the management team, who would know where I would be.

I look forward to continuing to work at IIL—I enjoy myself tremendously and believe that I can help grow this company to be (even more) successful and fruitful.

Hoping for $3 million by the close of this year.

All the best—
Michelle

Others of us "chimed in" to reinforce Robin's acknowledgment, as he copied just about everyone in the company on it—a special recognition in and of itself. One manager named Jeanie responded:

You know, Michelle.... Robin is right. You have done an outstanding job over the past few years. It is fun to watch you grow, both in your sales expertise AND as a young lady!!!! We are all proud of you and I consider it a privilege to work with you.

KEEP UP THE GREAT WORK!!!!!!

Regards,
Jeanie

I also (naturally) added my "two cents" and copied everyone as well:

Robin has so eloquently described Michelle's well-deserved success. Please add my congratulations to his. Michelle, you are a great role model in sales success for all of us! You have made and continue to make a great contribution to IIL.

Best,
Judy

And how long did it take Robin to write this "hang it on your wall in a silver frame" acknowledgment? Probably no more than a few minutes, yet the impact was profound both in terms of making Michelle feel wonderful and giving her even greater motivation to succeed, as you saw from her response.

The results of these kinds of actions that created the positive responses that you just read are even validated in current research, as reported by Barbara Fredrickson in a book entitled *The Psychology of Gratitude*: "Indirect evidence that positive emotions transform organizations and help them to thrive comes from research that links employee engagement to a wide range of organizational outcomes ... research shows that organizations with employees who experience frequent positive emotions have lower employee turnover, more customer loyalty, higher net sales, and in turn more profitable financial outcomes" (p. 159). Those are pretty good reasons, if you need a few, to start acknowledging the people you work with!

Sometimes a simple acknowledgment can lead to new business ideas. Here's an example of this. When someone brings in large revenues for our company, I often send an acknowledgment memo to them when I receive the report. On one occasion, when I saw the large number of dollars a salesperson had generated, I asked her which account it was. It turned out that she had sold our company's training services to a state's Department of Transportation.

"Wow!" I wrote, "That's a deal that salespeople in all the states should benchmark. Every state has a DOT!" I asked her to write it up for one of our companywide news alerts. Would she have distributed this information on her own to key people on our team? Perhaps. But the acknowledgment led to it being done, and possibly to revenues generated that might not otherwise have been brought in to the company by our salespeople.

So you can send e-mails, or fax letters to acknowledge people at work. But you can also do some fun and far-out things as well to recognize their contribution or success. I love the following idea, which comes from the website of a company I have worked with for several years:

"Typically when you hear a gong it means you have to get off the stage. But at Imagination, we can't wait for that sound. When the president starts banging the giant gong that sits in our conference room, we all stop what we're doing, grab our champagne glasses, and herd into the room for some bubbly and toast to new business.

Overboard? Maybe. But the gong ceremony means that all of our hard work and diligence has just earned us a new client. And we use this quirky celebration to pat each other on the back for it. It's one of the many ways that we stay connected and motivated."

In other words, through the power of acknowledgment! In these simple, little ways, we can change the world of work for someone. If we all do it on a regular basis, we can change the workplace for many someones! Take the time. It's worth the effort.

Chapter 5

Overcoming the Obstacles to Acknowledgment and Reaping the Rewards

Principle #5: Truthful, heartfelt and deserved acknowledgments always make a difference, sometimes a profound one, in a person's life and work.

Rarely given acknowledgments have no more value than frequent ones. Sincere praise should not be withheld due to fear of diminishing returns, of appearing inappropriate or out of embarrassment. These obstacles can and should be overcome in order for you and your recipients to reap the tremendous rewards.

Why do people withhold acknowledgments in the first place? One reason is the myth that too much of a good thing devalues its worth. The second reason, also a myth, is that people value praise more if they rarely receive it.

Let's start by looking at the too-much-of-a-good-thing belief a little more closely. Imagine that your spouse or partner tells you every day with absolute sincerity how wonderful and incredible you are. Does that make you appreciate this deeply felt acknowledgment any less? Assuming that the statement is truthful and comes from the heart, it will be greatly valued and appreciated.

In a work environment, the myth may feel like it has a little more weight. People could well believe that too much acknowledgment cheapens its intent and devalues its meaning. The way to prevent this outcome is to both acknowledge quality work freely and generously and be (almost) equally forthright about giving constructive criticism. It is the balance and, above all, the truthfulness that gives your acknowledgments power.

I saw this in action when our company became a sponsor of the newly created "International Project Management Day" in 2005, the first of what is now an annual day of recognition for and, yes—acknowledgment of—project managers around the globe. Although we had gotten involved as a sponsor very near to the actual date, I thought it would be wonderful to get New York City's Mayor Michael R. Bloomberg to declare it International Project Management Day throughout the city of New York. Normally, it takes six months to a year to get a proclamation to happen, assuming, of course, that the Mayor's staff thinks it is a good idea. We only had six weeks.

I asked my associate, Michelle (a different Michelle from the person I mentioned previously), if she were up for a nearly impossible challenge. She jumped at the opportunity. Although she received rejection after rejection, she kept on pushing. In about three weeks, she had worked the proclamation possibility up to a "well, maybe" and by the fourth week she got the "yes!"

It had been such a long shot, that I had sworn her to secrecy, and we hadn't told anyone what she was up to, including our CEO. When we got the yes, I told my boss and everyone I could find in the office that day, that Michelle had accomplished the nearly impossible. I acknowledged her perseverance, her persistence, her unflappability in the face of rejection. A companywide news alert went out both in our United States headquarters and to our foreign companies, acknowledging the accomplishment, which was picked up by our industry's most important trade publication.

The proclamation was framed and "unveiled" at a reception held by our company at a major hotel. We were *thrilled* with Michelle's accomplishment and wanted her to know it from her head to her feet.

Do you think she grew tired of all of the acknowledgments she received from our CEO and from me, as well as from others? Fat chance. She savored them. For this year's celebration, she has already gotten the "yes" from Mayor Bloomberg for another New York City proclamation, and is now working on having it proclaimed International Project Management Day throughout New York State and in other high places. So acknowledging Michelle not only made her feel good, but made her motivated to accomplish even more than she had previously. Our company, our employees and the event itself will certainly benefit from the extra enthusiasm that came from her being acknowledged.

People also hold back on acknowledgment in a work environment either because they are too busy and just don't get around to it, because they are embarrassed, or because they feel that it takes away a person's motivation and desire to strive to be better. *Au contraire!*

Acknowledgment diminishes resentment and lethargy, while building enthusiasm, focus, excitement and commitment. Acknowledgment and striving go together. When people feel validated through acknowledgment, they can't be stopped. They will bend over backwards, working massive overtime or go to great lengths if necessary, to get the job done the best they possibly can.

I have experienced this very clearly in my own work. As the publisher of a Web portal for 35,000 project managers in 90 different countries, I create a monthly newsletter that I always strive to make a great resource for our members. The work involved is continuously intense, and I feel a great obligation to our members to make it as valuable, readable, and fun a resource as I can. And I *live* for the feedback I receive, most of which is usually positive and/or constructive. One month, however, I got *no* feedback whatsoever and found myself becoming irritable, depressed and lethargic over the prospect of pulling together the next month's newsletter, an arduous task even when I was in a *good* frame of mind.

"Why should I put so much into it when people don't even care?" I whined to myself.

So when the time came to write my publisher's letter, the first feature of the newsletter, I decided to take a big and rather unconventional editorial risk. I started my letter to many thousands of people all over the globe with the following: "I'm depressed," I wrote, "and it's *your* fault!"

I then went on to explain how devastating it was to put so much work into something and receive no response. I really vented. At the bottom of the letter I mentioned that it just happened to be my birthday (the day the publication was being electronically distributed). I then sat back... and waited, fearful that I would still get no feedback.

Just minutes after the key was pressed to send the newsletter out, the responses started pouring in. People apologized for only taking and not giving back. They told me what a phenomenal goldmine our publication was for them. I learned of additional resources people had gotten for their company projects by showing their bosses articles we had published. I received promises of participation and contribution to our global community of project managers. And I received electronic birthday cards, birthday poems, and acknowledgments galore. I have never experienced that amount and degree of acknowledgment for my work in my life.

For weeks afterward, the acknowledgments kept coming, in response to my rather "direct" communication. This experience increased my determination to deliver the best material possible, no matter what amount of effort it took. Had I received no responses to my communication, I would have thrown in the emotional towel immediately and the professional towel as soon as I was able to do so. But instead, the acknowledgments made me thrive, as well as strive to be and do better. There was no such thing as diminishing returns for me in that situation!

Besides the myth of diminishing returns when it comes to acknowledging others, there are additional obstacles that get in the way of free, easy and appropriate acknowledgments. One of these is embarrassment. Either you feel shy about making the acknowledgment or you sense that the recipient will be made very uncomfortable by it. Maybe the person is shy, too. Or perhaps you're worried because he or she is senior to you and you fear your response will be seen as inappropriate or as "sucking up" in a way that will make you both uncomfortable.

I remember a time when I felt this concern. Years ago, the CEO of my company and I were at the annual conference of our professional trade association. I had been with the company for about eight years at the time, and had watched it grow at a tremendous pace. During a special session for international project managers, all of our company's global offices were represented and our people were asked to stand up. I felt a surge of pride as I saw our staff members from around the world be recognized.

With just a minor concern about being seen as

"brown-nosing," I scribbled a note to my boss, telling her how much pleasure it gave me to see representatives from all of our different foreign companies at the session, and how proud I was to be a part of the organization. I gave it to her, she smiled and nodded, and then we went on to other things. What I didn't find out until many years later was that she had pocketed the note and has it tucked away to this day, treasuring it as a reminder of the distance our company has come. I wrote the note with little fear of being perceived as "sucking up," because it was totally truthful. Therefore it landed as I wanted it to, and with even more meaning than I ever could have imagined.

We never know how much an acknowledgment will mean to another, and what a difference it will make in their lives and spirits. That's why it is worth the possible embarrassment or risk of being seen as inappropriate—as long as it is honest and real. My boss was moved and inspired by my note, but only because she trusted absolutely that what I had written came from my heart.

Some people are great at acknowledging certain levels of people in the workplace, but not others—even when the others deserve it. I recently heard about a senior manager in the publishing industry who was extremely generous with her acknowledgments of junior staff members, but stingy with praise of the top level executives who reported to her. The person who related the incident to me told me of the senior staff's great embarrassment when they admitted to each other (and she was one of them) how much they *craved* the manager's praise. Somehow, this was "leaked" to the manager and she was astounded. "But you know I respect all of your work, and I'm sure you know how much I value you!" she said emphatically. It had never occurred to her, though, that her top people needed the acknowledgment as much as the junior staff members. The executive who described the need told me that she is now in a senior position herself, and that she goes out of her way to acknowledge the high-ranking as well as the junior people who report to her. The payoff she sees is the wonderful effects of her praise on people of all levels, all of the time.

Now let me ask you a key question: How often have you heard that a rarely given acknowledgment is much more valuable than one that is frequently given? Too often, I would say! The theory is that if a person rarely acknowledges others, then when they do, they must really mean it and so its worth is increased. This is a myth! While I certainly am not advocating that you acknowledge others when you don't mean it or feel it, I am suggesting that when you feel that someone has done something wonderful or worthwhile, that you don't just note it to yourself but that you deliver it to the person without self-censorship, whenever the spirit moves you.

Of course acknowledgments, if they are to have an impact, must be *authentic*. Otherwise, they are worthless. And they must also be balanced with constructive criticism as appropriate, or else the acknowledgments could lose their impact. If balanced and truthful, frequency—even from someone not generally known to give them—cannot diminish their value. Yes, I know that when I receive a compliment or an acknowledgment from a senior colleague who does not give them very often, that it is worth a great deal. But what about all the time I have spent worrying about how I am being perceived and whether I am doing a good enough job? I think my concerns would be alleviated, and my performance—without the distraction of worry—might actually be improved, if he or she let me know on a more regular basis what they see as my worth and contribution to the organization.

You may be thinking that an acknowledgment must be eloquent or dramatic, powerful or remarkable, or moving and exceptional in order to have an effect on the person you deliver it to. You might assume that much thought must go into it, some preparation and a lot of courage. None of this is actually necessary in order for it to have an enormous impact. Sometimes a simple, quiet acknowledgment can make a profound difference in a person's life and the direction of their whole career. My brother, Carl, who is a highly respected podiatrist in the state of California, has been co-directing the Baja Project for Crippled Children—which has treated and operated on over 1,700 infants and children with severe congenital and acquired deformities such as clubfeet— for more than a quarter of a century. The Project serves indigent children in Mexico, El Salvador and Honduras. This involves trips of over 500 miles on the average of once a month, as well as away missions for three to five days at a time. As the years have gone by it has gotten harder and harder for Carl to make the trips; harder to keep the eight key members of the project's medical team involved on a continuous basis; and harder to find medical residents to accompany them.

In 2005, on an exhausting, whirlwind trip to Honduras, Carl treated a five-year-old child named Scarlet, who had been born with a deformed foot growing out of her thigh. She had never walked without crutches, and couldn't attend school because of the painful ridicule she experienced. Even with her physical limitations, on the day of surgery Scarlet practically jumped onto the operating table and pulled the gas mask down over her own face (most children fought it). My brother then surgically amputated the useless foot and leg above the knee, and made arrangements for a prosthesis to be provided for her through the generosity of the Honduran doctors and government. After treating her, and many other patients he operated on during the five day surgical tour, Carl left—totally wiped out and dog-tired. Although he had always experienced the joy of making a difference in the lives of infants and children who otherwise could not have afforded such services, when it came time to plan the next trip to Honduras, he began to ask himself why he kept doing this. Maybe, he thought, it was finally time to stop or at least seriously cut down on these missions of mercy.

Several months passed and he still had not booked the next trip. And then one day, Carl received an email from an attending doctor in the Honduras clinic, taken on the colleague's cell phone. Along with his message of appreciation to Carl for making Scarlet's first steps without crutches possible, my brother saw the photo of the child standing on *two* legs for the first time, one with a prosthesis—an incredible miracle. But what he saw most clearly from the photo was the total joy radiating from her face, which reached directly into his heart. Had that doctor not taken the time to send the photo as an acknowledgement of my brother's life-altering work, there might have been an outcome considerably different from what actually occurred.

Soon after receiving the photo, Carl booked the next grueling trip to Honduras. During that visit, Scarlet was brought in to see him. She walked quickly (without crutches) to him, then jumped into his arms, giving him a gigantic hug and kiss.

"The result of seeing her created warmth that swept over me, from head to toe," Carl said emotionally. "It absolutely recreated my desire, my will, and my need to do more."

Carl is a perfect example of how we push past our limits when we feel the degree to which we make a difference in the lives of others and are valued for it.

Ultimately, life and work are all about our actions and how they are received. Acknowledgments make us thrive—they give life to our spirit. There can never be too many of them.

Chapter 6

The Surprising Health Benefits of Acknowledgment

Principle #6: It is likely that acknowledgments can improve the emotional and physical health of both the giver and the receiver.

There is already substantial scientific evidence that gratitude and forgiveness help well-being, alertness and energy, diminish stress and feelings of negativity, actually boosting the immune system. It is reported that they can even reduce the risk of stroke and heart failure. This research leads us to believe that acknowledging others has similar effects.

After reading this book in rough draft form, "my brother the doctor" said that it changed the frequency and depth of his acknowledgments of his children, his staff and his wife. I was delighted, of course, and then asked him to describe as accurately as possible how he physically felt as he acknowledged these people. "What I experience when I acknowledge someone," he said, "especially when it's an acknowledgment I would normally withhold, is a kind of release. It feels like it does when I sigh deeply. It is like a pressure being released from within, a kind of calm. . . ."

It seems that Carl is describing first hand what is emerging from current scientific research, which is lending support to the idea that acknowledgment is healthy and beneficial for both the giver and the receiver.

Researchers have already discovered that gratitude—a kind of inward form of acknowledgment—helps people's sense of well-being, level of alertness and energy. A 2003 study that was conducted by University of California, Davis psychology professor Robert Emmons and University of Miami psychology professor Michael E. McCullough focused on the effects of gratitude on physical and emotional well-being.

The participants in this study were 201 health psychology undergraduate students in a large, public university. The subjects were split into three groups:

"Well-being," "Hassle/Irritants" and "Neutral," or the control group. The well-being group was instructed to list in their journal five things that they were grateful or thankful for that week. The hassle or irritant group was instructed to list five things they found annoying in their journals and the third group was simply instructed to write five things that had impacted them during the week. Along with the weekly journals, the subjects were asked to complete a general health checklist with symptoms including loss of appetite, headache, nausea and weakness.

This study concluded that the people who practiced gratitude rated their live's more favorably and experienced fewer symptoms of physical illness, such as stress and fatigue.

Since gratitude is both the state from which a person acknowledges another (e.g., "I'm grateful for what you have done for me, for our project, or for our company and therefore I acknowledge your contribution"), as well as the positive and grateful response of the recipient, these findings should apply to acknowledgment as well as gratitude.

Psychologist Rita Justice, Ph.D. reported on the interactions between mind and body in a 2003 article in the University of Texas Houston Health Leader newsletter:

"Researchers have found that when we think about someone or something we really appreciate and experience the feeling that goes with the thought, the parasympathetic—calming-branch of the autonomic nervous system is triggered. This pattern when repeated bestows a protective effect on the heart." Perhaps this is related to the feeling of "calm" cited by my brother that was associated with the giving of acknowledgments.

Aside from the important contributions we make when we acknowledge people, the evidence of the positive physiological effects for both giver and receiver in the growing field of "psychoneuroimmunology" are being documented on a continuous basis. If you Google this term, you get links to hundreds of thousands of articles and research studies reporting on or showing evidence for these kinds of connections. While it is not my intent in this book to prove the case scientifically for the health benefits of acknowledgment, it *is* my desire to give you just a little more motivation and ammunition to start acknowledging *many* people on a regular basis!

A personal example of the possible health benefits of acknowledgment seemed to occur when I was working extremely hard, but feeling really inadequate, stressed out and discouraged about a new project I had undertaken. In the midst of my frustration and hopelessness, I received an e-mail from our head of sales, Lori, telling me how quickly I had grasped what needed to be done, how well I was going about doing it and that she was sure I would be successful within a short time.

The result of that e-mail? I remember feeling exhilarated and rejuvenated after reading Lori's words, and immediately got back on the phone with enthusiasm and the intention of creating results.

Perhaps even more important, I vividly recall feeling physically different after reading it! If you'd measured my stress hormones afterward, they probably would have dropped, along with my blood pressure and pulse rate.

In fact, I think I became a textbook example of a study that was described in an article in the American Journal of Cardiology (McCraty et al, 1995). This work suggests that appreciation and other positive emotions lead to alterations in the electrical activity of the heart that, in turn, may be beneficial in the treatment of high blood pressure and in preventing the likelihood of sudden death in patients with congestive heart failure and coronary artery disease!

Those findings dramatically show the impact we can have on each other's health and well-being on a day to day basis. So when you see the opportunity to give the kind of encouragement that Lori gave to me, to someone in your life, take the extra minute. You'll bring energy, excitement, and probably a healthier state of being to yourself as well as to the other person.

Chapter 7

Acknowledging the People Who Matter to You

Principle #7: Practice Different Ways of Getting Through to the People You Want to Acknowledge.

Develop an acknowledgment repertoire that will give you the tools to reach out to the people in your life in the different ways that will be the most meaningful to each situation and each person.

Are you starting to get a better understanding of why many people don't acknowledge others freely or frequently, and of the positive effects of acknowledgment on those around you? I hope so, because I would love for us to get busy changing the lives of people throughout the world for the better right now.

To help you begin practicing and enhancing your acknowledgment skills, I am providing you with a list of suggested people in your daily life to consider acknowledging. You may also need to know what to do when people won't accept your gift. This is infrequent, but it is bound to happen from time to time, since you will be giving so many of them. So here are a few thoughts to help you deal with this situation should it occur.

Some people have such a negative image of themselves, or are just so distracted, that they are unable to hear your wonderful words of praise. You will feel like you have thrown a boomerang: It will come right back to you and you will feel stuck with it.

When this has happened to me, I have touched the person's arm or made very direct eye contact, and then said something like, "I just told you how deeply I appreciated your working so many hours of overtime to get our project completed, but I don't feel like you really heard me. I don't think you 'got' what I was trying to communicate to you, and it's important to me that you get it!"

Usually, the person seems to wake up—his or her eyes refocus and open wider, they might tilt their head back a bit, as if they are actively listening. Then I repeat the acknowledgment and usually this time they get it. I have even gone to acknowledgment delivery #3 a few times (I can be rather obnoxious in my commitment to their "getting" it), and I assure you that it is well worth the repetition when you see the broad smile, the light in their eyes, and even tears sometimes, as I saw when my friend finally let in my acknowledgment about what a good mother she was.

So now that you are prepared for all kinds of responses and reactions, let's start the process by making a few lists. This will help you organize the process and make it easier to get started:

1. People to acknowledge in my daily life and what I could say to acknowledge them.

    a. coffee shop person _____

    b. car mechanic _____

    c. dry cleaner _____

    d. bank teller _____

    e. mail deliverer _____

    f. doctor _____

    g. dentist _____

h. child's teacher _____

i. _____

j. _____

k. _____

2. People in my family and what I could say to acknowledge them:

a. husband/wife _____

b. child 1 _____

c. child 2 _____

d. mother _____

e. father _____

f. brother/sister _____

g. grandmother _____

h. grandfather _____

i. mother-in-law _____

j. father-in-law _____

k. _____

l. _____

m. _____

3. People at work and what I could say to acknowledge them:

a. boss (don't rule this out due to FOBN—"fear of brown-nosing." If the acknowledgment is real for you, it will be perceived that way.)

b. subordinate 1 _____

c. subordinate 2 _____

d. subordinate 3 _____

e. co-worker 1 _____

f. co-worker 2 _____

g. co-worker 3 _____

h. mailroom assistant _____

i. office manager _____

j. client 1 _____

k. client 2 _____

l. _____

m. _____

n. _____

Once you have filled these out, start finding opportunities to deliver them. They can be acknowledgments that you write, or verbally present, or they can be something quite different. As long as the acknowledgments are true and real for you, acknowledge away. Here are some examples of acknowledgments that may help get you started, and also make you more aware of the incredible power that acknowledgments can have.

The first example is one I referred to in an earlier chapter that I predicted would "knock your socks off." It is an illustration of the power of acknowledgment of public employees, how it deeply affects them and helps make the world more workable. About a year ago, my daughter—the young lady who, as a child, gave those wonderful manicures to elderly ladies in a nursing home—took a seriously wrong turn and ended up in the jurisdiction of Drug Court, a phenomenal program that presents the choice to addicts of having either a jail sentence or serious drug rehabilitation.

Once officially in the program and in residential rehab, my daughter Stefanie quickly got herself kicked out of the rehab program, and was being sentenced to jail until another, more rigorous program could be found. A driver from the original rehab program was escorting her to the County Courthouse for sentencing, but was not allowed to take her inside. She would just have to be left at the door until someone from the court could pick her up.

When my husband and I heard about this, we were extremely worried that she was a "flight risk" and would take off. Not knowing what else to do, I called the County Courthouse. A wonderfully helpful man named George answered the phone and once he knew the situation, started making calls on my daughter's behalf until he found someone who would meet her at the door and take her inside at the approximate arrival time.

I was so appreciative of George's effort that I wrote a letter to his boss, the Chief Clerk of the County Courthouse.

After explaining the situation that had occurred, I wrote, "George B., who just happened to answer the phone that day, made some calls to help assure our daughter's safe keeping. He went out of his way to be supportive and helpful, and in that dreadful situation I can't begin to tell you how much it meant to talk to a real human being who wanted to help. . . I wanted you to know how much it meant to us on that terribly unsettling day, to find someone who just happened to answer the phone and who exhibited true concern and interest. I think George B. should be officially acknowledged and held up as a role model for people who deal with the public. He made a tremendous difference at a very difficult time."

I sent the letter off and shortly after that received an e-mail from George's boss stating the following:

I have been employed by the Office of Court Administration for twenty one years. In my experience most individuals that have comments about the staff are negative comments. Rarely do individuals take the time to compliment workers for doing their jobs and going that extra bit to assist the public. I wanted to thank you for acknowledging one of my workers, George B., for taking the time to assist you and your family in a challenging period. His efforts obviously were of great value to you and helped you. I am proud of the work that my staff does because it often is thankless and they receive little attention for a difficult job. Sometimes a little positive feedback motivates employees and then it become contagious and a better workplace develops. I wish you and your family the best of luck...

I also received an e-mail from George B., himself, in which he said:

Judy,

...I want to thank you for taking the time to write your letter to (my boss). It is hard to describe how good something like that can make you feel. I didn't consider it a major effort to help you with your situation back in November; it's just something I tried to do to alleviate your anxiety that day ...Very few (people) take the time to let our bosses know that we have done something that someone perceives as special. I think human nature makes us hope that we will be noticed for the things we do.

... It's hard to think that the things we do in life, especially the good, is often ignored. It is always good to get a pat on the back, be it figuratively or literally. It makes you walk just a bit off the ground for a day or even more. Thanks for providing that feeling for me.

... I wish only good things for you and your family.

I feel certain that if people like George get acknowledged for the helpful things that they try to do, maybe on a daily basis, that they would do more of them! As George told us, it is only human nature, and it would make all of our lives work so much more smoothly and gracefully, if we all did this.

And by the way, Stefanie is doing much better in a different drug rehab program and is remembering more and more of her original desire to acknowledge and contribute to others. And by the way, she has urged me to be direct about this experience and not to try to fudge or hide the details as I described them it to you. I have honored her request in the hope that the complete anecdote will motivate you to acknowledge public servants who are truly helpful, and for all of us to assist in making the world work better!

Here's another example of the power of acknowledgment. This occurred when I was working for my television client, Yue-Sai Kan, earlier in my career. At the time, she was the host and executive producer of two television series that promoted understanding between Eastern and Western cultures, and I was very proud of her accomplishments. I had gotten wind of awards to be given out by the Better World Society, a group started in the 1980's by the glamorous celebrity Ted Turner, to acknowledge people that were making contributions to global peace and prosperity. Turner, who chaired the organization, would be presenting the awards.

I furtively filled out the submission form, clearly stating the major contribution Ms. Kan had made to global understanding and communications with her two television series "Looking East," which aired on various American cable networks and "One World," broadcast on China Central Television (CCTV). I wrote that her efforts toward bridging the cultures of East and West were estimated to have reached a worldwide audience of over 400 million people each week. I had such a clear sense of her winning the award, that in my mind I actually "saw" her graciously accepting it from Ted Turner! When she received notification that she *had* won the award, Yue-Sai was a little shocked to find out that I had acknowledged her by secretly nominating her for the honor. The star-studded event was held at the Waldorf Astoria and attended by celebrities such as Jane Alexander, Ben Vereen, Phil Donahue and Jean-Michel Cousteau.

This was a powerful experience not just for Yue-Sai, who received great publicity and further acknowledgment from many influential people, but for me as well. It involved totally trusting not just my desire to acknowledge someone I greatly admired, but trusting my vision— in this case, seeing her "accept" the prestigious award from Ted Turner as I filled out the submission form.

It told me that when I had mental pictures or visualizations of this nature, I needed to follow my gut. This has served me well in both my career and my personal life.

One other demonstration of the power of acknowledgment occurred very recently. A close relative of mine has mid-stage Alzheimer's disease, and was convinced that someone had broken into her house and stolen a favorite skirt and other items of clothing. She wanted her husband to call the police, but he knew that this would be inappropriate and ineffective. I was aware of the Alzheimer's Association's 24/7 helpline, and so I called to support my relative, not having any idea what could possibly make the situation better. The person on the phone, a lovely woman named Elizabeth, was so helpful and insightful that she was able to totally diffuse the situation by talking to my relative and letting her know that she was safe, which turned out to be her major concern. My relatives were both so grateful for her dedication and service that I wrote the following note to a key person in the Association, asking that Elizabeth be acknowledged by someone in authority in the organization:

Dear Maria,

I just want to let your organization know what an incredible service it provides through its 24/7 helpline. Two nights ago (a close relative) called me in a very upset state, as (his wife), who has mid-stage Alzheimer's, was frantic and terribly anxious about some things that she believed had been stolen from their apartment. She wanted him to call the police, but he knew that the items (a skirt, etc.) had just been misplaced. She kept insisting on it, so he called me to help. I then called the 800 number, and a simply superb person by the name of Elizabeth walked and talked us through it. She actually spoke to my relative and got to the root of her concerns, assured her and then reassured her and through some very creative and bold intervention, solved the problem entirely.

I can't thank your organization enough for having this service, and I want you to know that you are all very fortunate (as is my family) to have someone as compassionate, understanding and creative as Elizabeth as an information specialist and helpline responder. I hope your management will acknowledge her for the service that she provided to my family during a very difficult situation.

I thank all of you from the bottom of my heart for being there when we needed you.

Warm regards,
Judy Umlas

Soon after I sent the letter, I got a call from Maria, thanking me for taking the time to acknowledge a worker of theirs, and she also let me know how much it meant to all of them to receive my words of praise about one of these dedicated people. She said she would make sure that Elizabeth was appropriately acknowledged for her outstanding service to our family. Then, to my delight, she asked if the association could publish my letter of acknowledgment in their upcoming newsletter, in order to let people know more about their services and how valuable they had been to our family. I was thrilled, gave my permission of course, and hope that the letter will encourage others to take advantage of such an important and helpful service in their own challenging situations. The acknowledgment turned out to be a win for all concerned.

So remember, you gain at least as much as—if not more than—the recipients, from giving acknowledgments. You simply don't know the full force and power of acknowledgment until you start using it, bravely, courageously and on a daily basis!

When you begin to write or verbalize acknowledgments such as the ones I have shared with you, watch the people around you wake up, come alive, and have more energy! And you are creating that. Once you see the power of acknowledgment, you won't want to stop using it. Do it until it becomes second nature to you. And imagine a world where everyone feels deeply acknowledged for who they are and what they contribute.

I have created this book as a simple but, I hope, potent call to action for us all. And I personally acknowledge every one of you who has read this book, for being up to the challenge of making excellent use of the power of acknowledgment to light up the world, one person at a time!

In Closing...

As I opened this book with its dedication to my cherished friend, Barbara Leach-Kelly, I will close it with a letter that she wrote to me a few months before she died. I have read this letter over and over again, and it has meant the world to me to have it. Her acknowledgment has brought me peace, solace and the ongoing warmth of her love. I believe she must have known at the time she wrote it what the power of this acknowledgment would be for me—then and forever.

On June 14, 2005

Dear Judy,

Happy...happy birthday!! You have been a blessing from God this year and I could not have made it through without your love and selflessness. May the light of God and the love of life be yours always. Please know you have made a difference in the quality of my life and strength of my heart, and I thank you. I love you dearly.

Barbara

Thank you, Barbara! And I leave all of you...for now...with the request that you make sure that every person in your life who matters to you knows how important they are to you. And at the same time, I request that you acknowledge everyone else around you for everything good that you observe in them. You will see ALL of these people light up, and the world will indeed be a brighter and happier place for all of us!

References

EMMONS, R., McCULLOUGH, M., 2003. "Counting blessings versus burdens: An experimental investigation of gratitude and subjective well-being in daily life." *Journal of Personality and Social Psychology.* Volume 84, No. 2, p. 377-380.

FREDRICKSON, B. L. *The Psychology of Gratitude.* New York: Oxford University Press, 2004.

JUSTICE, R. Ph.D. "The effects of joy and gratitude on the human body." *Health Leader,* 2003, http://www.healthleader.uthouston.edu/archive/Mind_Body_Soul/2003/givingthanks-1124.html

McCRATY, R., et al, 1995. "The effects of emotions on short-term power spectrum analysis of heart rate variability." *American Journal of Cardiology.* Volume 76, Issue 14, p. 1089-1093

Author's Personal Acknowledgments

In this book on "The Power of Acknowledgment," I find it ironic that it is so hard for me to write my personal acknowledgments. I think that's because there are so many people who have contributed to me on my journey that I can't possibly list them all. But here is an abbreviated list.

I acknowledge my family for all the love and support they have given me. I especially want to thank my grandmother, Lena Handler, for introducing me to the power of acknowledgment when I was a child. It has stayed with me always.

I acknowledge my dear friends Barbara Leach-Kelly; Kayli and Jerry Goldman and their two wonderful sons, Scott and David; Jerry and Carol Goldin; my precious friend for 34 years, Susan Ellen Spar Adams, Esq.; and my good friend, Dr. Rita Ghiraldini, for their patience, kindness, caring, continuous love and encouragement, their support and contribution.

I acknowledge my three incredible mentors, coaches, supporters in my professional life. In chronological order there is Peter Kohler, who believed in me, challenged me and encouraged me to write professionally at WCBS-TV, even though I had to rewrite my first television editorial 13 times!

Then there is Yue-Sai Kan, one of the most professionally daring and exciting people I have worked for. She challenged me with wonderfully impossible tasks, saw to it that I achieved them and always told me how resourceful I was.

And last, but certainly not least, E. LaVerne Johnson, the CEO and visionary of IIL and my personal partner in turning vision into reality in record time. It has been a great honor to work with her for the past 15 years. I thank her from the bottom of my heart for believing in me, and in this book, and for supporting me totally in making this book the best it can be.

I also want to acknowledge Associate Publisher, Michelle Blackley, for her immeasurable patience with the endless drafts I submitted and her never-ending smiles and great attitude.

I want to thank my book designer, Tony Meisel, for his constant and continuing efforts (up to the very last possible minute) to make this book both beautiful and readable. I think he has succeeded wonderfully!

I want to thank Julia Kagan, the excellent editor I found again, 22 years after she edited my article for *Working Woman Magazine,* who so magnificently polished that text and made it sing! Hopefully her editing of this book has had a similar effect!

I also want to thank writer/editor Lynn Lauber, who gave me the first professional feedback on the manuscript when I dared to show it to her, and who encouraged me to move forward.

I want to acknowledge the friend I made on the way to Paris when I went with my son Jared, Lisa Shambro. She turned out to be incredibly supportive of this book project by assembling a focus group of people who did not know me to comment on the book.

I thank the people Lisa assembled for their honest and constructively critical feedback: You all encouraged me to make important changes which, I hope, made this a much better book than it would otherwise have been.

I want to acknowledge and thank all of the people at IIL who have given me their support by reading this book, giving me their honest feedback and providing me with many of the anecdotes that helped me drive home the major points I wanted to make. I would especially like to thank Frank P. Saladis, PMP, for being my co-publisher of allPM.com, the global web portal for project managers, and for creating the concept of International Project Management Day.

And I acknowledge everyone else who has served and supported me through the exciting journey of my life—people who emerge every day, as I do whatever I do.

In conclusion, I acknowledge every one of you who has picked up this book and put it to use. If you have read it, I will have the audacity to tell you that you will make positive changes in your life and in the lives of others. Thank you for being willing to do so and congratulations for making the world a better place!

About the Author

Judith W. Umlas is Senior Vice President, Learning Innovations at International Institute for Learning (IIL), a global training company specializing in Project, Program and Portfolio Management, Microsoft® Project, Business Analysis and Six Sigma. She heads up eLearning training programming, including satellite broadcasts, webcasts and instructor-led online learning. She develops new business strategies to keep the company on the cutting edge of corporate learning.

She has been the Executive Producer of more than 25 global satellite broadcasts with such world renowned presenters as Dr. Joseph Juran, Dr. Harold Kerzner, Dr. Genichi Taguchi, Dr. Margaret Wheatley, Dr. Eli Goldratt, Joel Barker and CEO's of many Fortune 500 corporations. One of the satellite broadcast series drew an audience of 10,000 people as weekly participants.

Since its acquisition in 2002, Umlas has also been

Co-Publisher of allPM.com, the fast-growing global Project Management Web portal, which is owned and operated by IIL. Under her direction, many new features were created, such as the "PM Tip of the Day" with new, valuable tools, templates, and tips posted by subject matter experts on a daily basis. The Website now holds a consistent top four or five position in Google searches for project management, and the number two position for project manager. Under her leadership, membership has grown from 4,000 to over 35,000 members in 90 countries since she took on the role of Co-Publisher.

She also heads up IIL Publishing, New York—a division of International Institute for Learning--which produces high quality business and project management books that offer next-generation solutions to busy professionals.

Prior to joining International Institute for Learning, Judith Umlas spent 25 years in the television industry. At CBS, where she spent 12 years, she was producer/writer at flagship CBS owned station, WCBS-TV. She wrote, formulated and produced editorials for the station's management and won numerous awards for these programs. She also directed month-long station television projects on subjects of public importance.

Ms. Umlas later spearheaded programming efforts at a New York City public television station (WNYC-TV) designed to both raise significant dollars and bring in outstanding television programs to the station. Such services as Japan's Fuji Television Network and Italy's RAI Television brought their excellent programs to WNYC-TV during this campaign.

Following this, she served as Director of Sales for a national cable television network, where she worked with various global television producers, including the world famous Chinese television host/producer, Yue-Sai Kan. She later worked with Ms. Kan to promote, sell and develop television programming for The Discovery Channel and business television programs for PBS.

Judith Umlas has written for numerous publications, including Working Woman magazine, The New York Times, The Chicago Tribune and was Vice President of American Women in Radio & Television. She currently resides in Palisades, New York with her family.

Coming soon from
IIL Publishing, New York

Project Portfolio Management Tools and Techniques
By Parviz F. Rad, Ph.D. and Ginger Levin, Ph.D.

The Zen of Project Management
By George Pitagorsky, PMP

Positive Leadership in Project Management
by Frank P. Saladis, PMP

Project Management Poetry, Puzzles and Pictorials
Original poems and other works
by project managers around the globe